The site of Joseph Paxton's famous glasshouse at Chatsworth House, Derbyshire, is now occupied by a hedge maze. Although the maze was planted only in 1962 it is beautifully in keeping with the surrounding historic garden.

Mazes and Labyrinths

Adrian Fisher

A Shire book

Published in 2004 by Shire Publications Ltd,
Cromwell House, Church Street, Princes Risborough,
Buckinghamshire HP27 9AA, UK.
(Website: www.shirebooks.co.uk)

Copyright © 2004 by Adrian Fisher.
First published 2004.
Shire Album 418. ISBN 0 7478 0561 X.
Adrian Fisher is hereby identified as the author of this
work in accordance with Section 77 of the Copyright,
Designs and Patents Act 1988.

British Library Cataloguing in Publication Data:
Fisher, Adrian
Mazes and labyrinths. – (Shire album; 418)
1. Maze gardens 2. Labyrinths
I. Title
793.7'38
ISBN 0 7478 0561 X

Cover: *The hedge maze at Leeds Castle, Kent.*

ACKNOWLEDGEMENTS
The author and publishers acknowledge their debt to Dr Diana Kingham for her work
on the Shire Album *Mazes*, a precursor to this volume.
Illustrations are acknowledged as follows: Belvedere Plantation, page 30 (top); Adrian
Fisher: pages 1, 4, 6, 9, 11 (bottom), 12, 15 (top and centre), 17, 18 (all), 19 (both), 20, 21
(both), 22, 24 (all), 25 (top and bottom), 26 (both), 27 (both), 28 (both), 29 (both), 30
(bottom), 31 (all), 32 (both), 33 (all), 34 (both), 35 (top), 36 (all), 37 (all), 38 (both), 39
(both), 40, 41 (both), 42 (both), 44 (both), 46, 48, 49 (both), 50, 51, 53, 54, and front
cover; Adrian Fisher Mazes Ltd, pages 3, 43 (all); Georg Gerster, page 15 (bottom);
Hever Castle, page 35 (bottom); National Museum of Wales, page 7 (top); Jeff Saward,
pages 8, 10, 11 (bottom); Richard Scott, The Herb Farm, Sonning Common, page 25
(centre); Bo Stjernstrom, page 7 (bottom).

Printed in Malta by Gutenberg Press Limited, Gudja Road,
Tarxien PLA 19, Malta.

Contents

The mirror maze within the Hamburg Dungeon, Germany, conveys the gruesome atmosphere of that city's notorious house of correction.

What is a maze?

The concept of a maze is universally familiar, embedded somewhere in the mists of everyone's childhood memories. Often this may be no more than the idea of a confusing network of pathways.

Different countries and cultures have different images of the maze. In Britain, the archetypal form is a hedge maze, such as the famous one at Hampton Court. In Japan, people tend to think of wooden panel mazes, following the great Japanese maze craze of the 1980s. In the United States, cornfield maize mazes are the most familiar form.

Underlying these differing forms are the same puzzle-maze elements: a complex network of paths, with junctions, choices and dead-ends; twisting and deceptive paths weaving between tall barriers; and, finally, an elusive goal to be reached.

Mazes have existed for only about four hundred years, whereas labyrinths, from which they are descended, go back four thousand. Confusingly, the English words 'maze' and 'labyrinth' are often used interchangeably even though the two constructions are not entirely the same. A labyrinth implies a single path and ritual aspects, while a 'maze' is a puzzle, with junctions and choices. Since they have just one course to follow, labyrinths are described as 'unicursal', whereas mazes are 'multicursal' because they contain many different sections of pathways.

What labyrinths lack in puzzlement is often more than compensated for by their content and symbolism. Over the millennia, in different cultures and civilisations, they have represented journeys of conquest, sieges of cities, pilgrimages, courtship and fertility, death and rebirth, and the linear thread of time – the 'path of life'. Religious and communal processions have

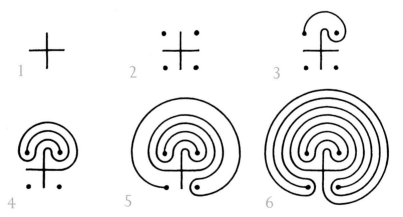

The construction of the seven-ringed classical labyrinth design. Start with a cross, add four dots, and then in turn connect each arm of the cross to its dot. This simple and memorable method of construction assisted widespread dissemination of the design around the world.

trodden their pathways; their coils have offered protection against evil spirits (which cannot easily go round corners) and symbolised the female womb, with the male seed penetrating and fertilising the egg and then emerging again as a newborn infant.

MYTHICAL ORIGINS

The earliest known labyrinth pattern is the classical (sometimes known as 'Cretan') design. Its seven rings of paths are easily created by drawing a cross and four dots and then joining them up to form eight concentric rings of barriers, leaving seven rings in between. This image has for many hundreds of years been carved on rocks and produced as full-sized turf and stone labyrinths throughout the world. Its specific man-made image and symbolic meanings are not to be confused with early spiral carvings, to which labyrinths bear a superficial resemblance.

The earliest and most famous labyrinth myth is the Greek legend of Theseus and the Minotaur. The Minotaur was born half man and half bull and was kept in a labyrinth designed by Daedalus for King Minos of Crete. Athens had lost a war to Crete and as a form of tribute was forced to send seven young men and seven maidens to be sacrificed to the Minotaur. Theseus, son of the king of Athens, volunteered himself as one of the group with the intention of killing the Minotaur and liberating Athens from the domination of Crete. King Minos's daughter Ariadne provided him with a ball of golden thread to unwind as he ventured through the labyrinth, thus enabling him to retrace his steps after the deed was done and find his way back out. Theseus entered the labyrinth, slew the Minotaur and escaped from Crete taking Ariadne with him. This is one of the most influential of the Greek myths. It has been kept alive over the centuries by labyrinths around the world, and through place-names, as well as by central mosaic images in Roman times.

Archaeological excavations of King Minos's palace at Knossos have revealed no trace of a labyrinth, although the extent and complexity of the palace buildings can certainly be described as labyrinthine. The *labrys* was the ritual double-headed axe of the Minoan civilisation on Crete during its zenith around 1700 BC, and thousands of these weapons have been excavated; this Greek word provides the origin for the word 'labyrinth'. The Minoans belonged to the powerful cult of the bull, and wall paintings in Knossos demonstrate acts of skill and bravery by athletes who leapt between the horns of fast-moving bulls. There are obvious parallels between the two sharp blades of the labrys and these pairs of pointed bovine horns. Sixteen hundred years later the labyrinth remained central to the island's culture, with the classical labyrinth pattern appearing on Cretan coins in the first century BC.

Ancient and medieval mazes

THE EARLIEST LABYRINTHS

Rock carvings are notoriously difficult to date and yet provide the earliest known representations of the labyrinth. The earliest classical labyrinth design could be a rock-art inscription in Galicia, north-west Spain, which has been tentatively dated to around 2000 BC. A vertical rock carving found in Sardinia is thought to have been created about 1600 BC, and a piece of Syrian pottery dated to around 1600 BC was inscribed with the labyrinth design. The oldest example in the British Isles is the Hollywood Stone, dated to about AD 550 and on display in the National Museum, Dublin.

ROMAN MOSAIC MAZES

The Romans took the classical labyrinth design and developed it in various ways to create mosaic labyrinths. Given the small scale of mosaic *tesserae* (the blocks that form Roman mosaics), labyrinth designs could be created with many more rings of paths than the original seven. Most Roman mosaic labyrinth designs are rectangular, since the pavements were installed indoors in square or oblong rooms, and the pieces of mosaic are effectively square. The designs involve tracing one entire quadrant at a time, usually proceeding clockwise around the design. The Roman mosaic industry was highly organised, with mosaics assembled in sections in specialised workshops, and these Roman designs, with their central illustrations, lent themselves to batch production of the four quadrants. The art form captured the imagination in all parts of the

One of two carvings of the classical labyrinth design in the Rocky Valley, Cornwall. It is carved into a vertical rock-face.

The incomplete Roman mosaic pavement discovered in the churchyard at Caerleon, Newport, is thought to date from the second or third century AD. Most Roman mosaic labyrinths are square in shape, since they were laid indoors in square or rectangular rooms.

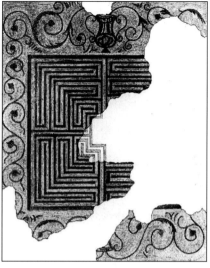

Roman Empire, with some fifty known examples created between 100 BC and AD 400.

Roman labyrinths were the first to employ imagery within their designs, although this was confined to one or more central images and a perimeter that typically portrayed a fortified city with turrets, towers and battlements. The themes most commonly chosen for central illustration were the siege of Troy and the legend of the Cretan labyrinth, the image of Theseus slaying the Minotaur being particularly popular. A square form of the classical design with the inscription *Labyrinthus hic habit Minotaurus* was found in Pompeii, scratched on a painted pillar.

Six Roman labyrinth mosaics have been found in Britain. One is in the Roman Legionary Museum at Caerleon, Newport. Another was found at Harpham, East Yorkshire; it measured 11 feet (3.4 metres) square and was displayed for a time in Hull City Hall.

STONE LABYRINTHS

Forms of construction are often dictated by the landscape and available materials; an ultimate challenge is presented in bare rocky coasts and islands scattered with loose strewn boulders. Around the shores of the Baltic there are over five hundred full-sized labyrinths made of stone boulders, many dating back to medieval times or

Below: A stone labyrinth of classical design with rows of boulders to form barriers between the paths. Mazes of this kind are found extensively along the shores of the Baltic Sea.

earlier. The boulders are lined up on the bare rock to form barriers, thus creating pathways in between.

There are many legends associated with these stone labyrinths, reflecting their maritime heritage. In past centuries fishermen would walk the paths of a labyrinth before putting to sea, believing this would ensure favourable winds and a good catch. If driven on to some distant shore during a storm the fisherman might build a labyrinth to contain and tame the fierce winds. The names of some of the places where such labyrinths are found are derived from the ancient cities of Troy, Jericho or Jerusalem, reflecting classical myths and biblical stories.

The oldest known British stone labyrinth was built in 1726 by the lighthouse keeper on St Agnes in the Scilly Isles. Also in the Scilly Isles, the earliest stone labyrinth on St Martin's was reputedly made by Second World War aircrew stationed on the island. There are a further fifteen modern stone labyrinths on St Martin's, although their positions and designs often change as visitors plunder one to construct another.

THE MEDIEVAL CHRISTIAN MAZE

The medieval Christian church recognised the power and symbolism of the labyrinth as an allegory for a spiritual journey and the 'path of life' and transformed it in two significant ways. First, the seven-ring classical pattern was superseded by a new eleven-ring medieval Christian design. Its most distinctive feature was that the paths crossed back on themselves on each of the principal axes, thus forming the unmistakable image of a cross; the paths also ranged freely through the quadrants rather than systematically through each quarter as in Roman mosaic labyrinths. Second, the labyrinth was brought indoors and laid in fine stone within the pavement floors of some of the greatest Gothic cathedrals in the world.

Chartres Cathedral in France contains the earliest medieval Christian pavement labyrinth (although the earliest example of the design appears on a manuscript dating from the tenth century). Known as *Chemin de Jerusalem*, it was built in 1235 at the same time as the present cathedral, with its three famous rose windows. It lies

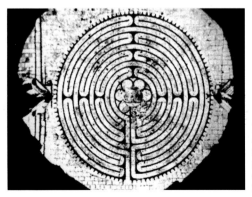

The pavement maze in Chartres Cathedral, France, showing the traditional medieval Christian design with its emphasised central cruciform motif. These pavement mazes were not built in English churches but the design is similar to that of many British turf mazes.

on the pavement floor in precise alignment with the western rose window, being the same circular shape and having the same diameter, and on the same central axis as the cathedral. From the threshold of the west door its centre is the same distance horizontally as the centre of the west window vertically. This precise hidden symbolism emphasises the significance of the labyrinth; it was an accessible physical path in two dimensions, compared with the glorious colour of the western rose window high above, visible but out of reach. The labyrinth represents the two-dimensional solidity of our mortal, temporal life; the shining rose window symbolises the promise of spiritual, eternal life. The name *Chemin de Jerusalem* reflected the recent journeys by the Crusaders to the Holy Land. Reaching the centre symbolised reaching both Jerusalem and salvation. Travelling to Chartres Cathedral and then tracing the labyrinth was a more accessible pilgrimage than the long and hazardous journey to Jerusalem itself.

In medieval times similar pavement labyrinths were laid in the floors of many other cathedrals, nearly all in northern France. There were two main forms of the design – circular (as at Chartres) or octagonal. Sometimes bastions were created in the four corners, to fill a square. No pavement labyrinths were created in English churches or cathedrals of the same period, although the distinctive eleven-ring medieval Christian design was later adopted in English turf mazes.

EARLY TURF MAZES

Turf mazes, like stone labyrinths, are one of the oldest forms of labyrinth. Again, they used the local material that was available, and their creators employed the simple method of digging a trench to form the dividing barrier, thus producing a dramatic raised pathway on which to walk. On chalk hilltops where the topsoil is thin, as in southern England, this construction spectacularly reveals the white chalk beneath.

This method is the opposite to what might have been expected, since it would have been much easier to cut a narrow trench for

The turf maze at Hilton, Cambridgeshire, located in a corner of the village green. The maze is 55 feet (17 metres) in diameter and is of nine-ring medieval Christian design; records show that it was formerly eleven-ringed. The present maze has at some time been recut incorrectly near the middle.

Plans of four lost turf mazes. (Top left) Robin Hood's Race at Sneinton, Nottinghamshire. (Top right) Walls of Troy in Holderness, East Yorkshire, was an unusually shaped maze some 40 feet (12 metres) in diameter. It was destroyed after 1815. (Bottom left) The turf labyrinth formerly in the parish of Pimperne, north Dorset, had the largest recorded turf maze, with a unique meandering design covering nearly an acre. Research suggests its precise location lay closer to Blandford. (Bottom right) The Shepherd's Race at Broughton Green, Northamptonshire, was destroyed by trench-digging practice by soldiers during the First World War.

walking in, in a manner resembling a narrow sheep path; indeed one walks in the gully at the Miz-maze near Winchester but this is an exception to the general rule.

Turf labyrinths were usually created in public places such as village greens and common land. As with maypole dancing and other May Day festivities, turf labyrinths are closely associated with the rites of spring, to celebrate renewed fertility after the winter. With the adoption of Christianity, springtime labyrinth traditions continued with the focus on Pentecost, the rebirth that is symbolised by confirmation and first communion.

Many speculative ideas surround Britain's enigmatic turf labyrinths, including this image of monks threading the turf maze at Sneinton, Nottinghamshire, on their knees as a form of religious penance.

Over two hundred place-names and locations of turf labyrinths have been identified across the British Isles, mainly in central and southern Britain, although only eight have survived; there are also a few extant examples in Germany and Poland. The earliest turf labyrinths had place-names such as 'Troy Town', 'Julian's Bower' and 'Maiden's Bower', reflecting similar pre-Christian themes to those of Scandinavian stone labyrinths. They followed the classical design, either directly with seven paths or with variations. The only two surviving classical examples are in a private garden at Somerton, Oxfordshire, and beside a road near Dalby, North Yorkshire. The name 'Miz-maze' is distinctive to southern England, whereas the names of the classical-style labyrinths are found more widely across Britain.

Europe's largest surviving ancient turf labyrinth lies on the common in Saffron Walden, Essex, and measures 132 feet (40 metres) across. Its paths are almost a mile in length.

The turf maze at Alkborough, Lincolnshire, offers an unmistakable clue that it is several centuries old. The entire area of pathways and gullies lies well below the level of the surrounding land as a result of repeated scouring out of the gullies over the years.

As Christianity spread, the church adapted existing culture in various ways. With turf labyrinths, the locations and place-names remained but the paths were recut in the medieval Christian design. All the other ancient turf mazes that have survived in Britain follow this design.

Early garden mazes

LOW BOX LABYRINTHS

Mazes with barriers of vegetation began to appear as ornamental garden features around the same time as knot gardens and parterres. Such features tended to be small and planted with low bushes close to the house so that they could be viewed from an upstairs window.

In France, King Charles V (reigned 1364–80) had a labyrinth within his pleasure garden at the Hôtel St Pol. It appears that by 1494 'a knot in a garden, called a mase' was a commonplace feature. These early planted mazes were usually unicursal in design and were not intended to confuse or provide a puzzle.

By the early seventeenth century dwarf box hedging was a popular choice for mazes because of its slow growth and longevity. At Hatfield House, Hertfordshire, Lady Salisbury created a twentieth-century maze in low box as part of the knot garden in front of the Old Palace; the surrounding raised walkway gives an excellent view across this knot garden.

FLORAL LABYRINTHS

Another kind of low-planted maze was the floral labyrinth. Here the barriers consisted of flower-beds containing plants, shrubs, fruit trees or herbs, typically edged with dwarf box. These were on a much larger scale than the low box labyrinths, forming a distinct area within the entire garden. They may have been similar in character to the twentieth-century Culpeper Garden at Leeds Castle, Kent.

Thomas Hill in his horticultural *Treatise* of 1568 gave two designs that could be used for mazes using low box hedges or set out as floral labyrinths. Hill recommended them as proper adornments for larger gardens, where they would provide recreation and decoration, and suggested planting fruit trees or 'Herbers decked with roses' in the corners and centre.

William Lawson's *A New Orchard and Garden* (1618) advised that a maze should be made of fruiting shrubs and trees 'well framed a

A circular design for a labyrinth, from Thomas Hill's 'Treatise' of 1568, which could be used for a low box-hedged maze or set out as a floral labyrinth.

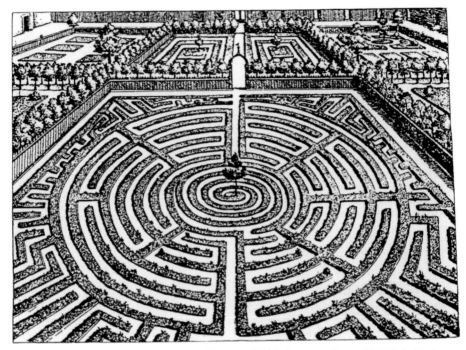

A design for a unicursal floral labyrinth from 'Hortorum Viridariorumque Formae' (1583) by Vredeman de Vries.

man's height so as to make your friend wander in gathering of berries till he cannot recover himself without your help'. In 2003 Randoll Coate created a modern orchard maze using trained fruit trees in a private walled garden for Sarah Callander-Beckett at Combermere Abbey near Whitchurch in Shropshire.

Sir William Brereton in 1634 described the new garden of Prince William of Orange in Holland as 'a remarkable garden in the shape of a square with high, trimmed hedges forming a maze'. The barriers, trained on strong wooden supports, consisted of evergreen and deciduous shrubs and fruit trees.

EARLY HEDGE MAZES

Mazes with barriers of tall hedges began to appear towards the end of the sixteenth century. In 1599 the maze at Nonsuch Palace, Surrey, was described as 'being set round with high plants so that one could neither go over nor through them'. Lord Burghley had a hedge maze at Theobald's in Hertfordshire at the same period, and its surviving design shows that it was unicursal.

The world's most famous hedge maze is at Hampton Court Palace near London. The hedging was planted between 1690 and 1695 by George London and Henry Wise on the instructions of King William of Orange, who had also created a hedge maze in 1682 at his royal palace at Het Loo in Holland. The Hampton Court maze has a

A plan of the tall hedge maze at Theobald's, Hertfordshire, shows it to have been a unicursal maze rather than a puzzle maze. The maze was destroyed in 1643 during the English Civil War.

distinctive trapezoid shape, dictated by the intersecting paths of the 'wilderness' area. Most importantly, it has various junctions and dead-ends – making it the world's oldest surviving example of a genuine puzzle maze.

Left and below: *The Hampton Court maze was created between 1689 and 1695. Its relatively simple design offers twice the puzzlement, since visitors must retrace their steps after reaching the goal.*

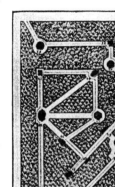

A plan of the Versailles labyrinth, France, drawn by Perrault (1677) shows that it was not a conventional hedge maze but one of the 'block' type, with statues and fountains placed at intervals.

PLAN DV
LABIRINTHE
DE VERSAILLES.

During the late seventeenth century, 'block' type mazes became popular in Holland, England and France. Here the hedges were no longer of uniform thickness but instead had winding paths penetrating large blocks of shrubs. Originally the puzzle hedge maze had been no more than a complex pattern of thin hedges within a given area; now it also offered an entertaining and diverting walk from one hidden feature to another. The Labyrinth of Versailles, constructed by J. Hardouin-Mansart for Louis XIV, was formed in this way and contained thirty-nine groups of statuary and fountains representing Aesop's *Fables*.

Block mazes were also popular in England. *Oxonia Depicta* illustrates an example at Trinity College, Oxford, but this one was little more than a series of open spaces linked by paths; it was destroyed in 1813. Kip's engravings of 1724 show block mazes at Belvoir Castle (Leicestershire), Boughton (Northamptonshire), Exton Park (Rutland), Badminton (Gloucestershire) and Castle Howard (North Yorkshire).

The Victorian revival

In Victorian times mazes increased in popularity in places of public amusement, such as at several pleasure gardens in London (Ranelagh Gardens, Vauxhall Gardens, White Conduit House in Islington and the celebrated Beulah Spa in south London), as well as in fashionable resorts.

PRIVATE ENTERTAINMENT

By the mid nineteenth century, tastes in private gardens were again swinging back to formality, and hedges, topiary and puzzle hedge mazes once more came into vogue.

An early pioneer of the revival was the fourth Earl Stanhope, who planted a maze at Chevening, Kent, between 1818 and 1830, to a design by the second Earl (1714–86), who was an eminent mathematician. His design was innovative, taking the art of maze design to the most complex two-dimensional form possible. Previously mazes had all their hedges ultimately linked to the perimeter hedge, making their solution relatively simple: by using the 'hand-on-wall' method of consistently turning right (or left) in and out of each dead-end, the goal could always be reached. The added complexity was achieved by siting the goal within a separate 'island' of hedges, so that visitors using the 'hand-on-wall' method could not reach the goal and eventually returned to the entrance.

The 'Italianate' style of gardening became popular in England during the 1830s and 1840s. The extensive Italian gardens at Shrublands Hall, Suffolk, created by Sir Charles Barry, included a hedge maze, which has been restored. An Italianate maze at Capel

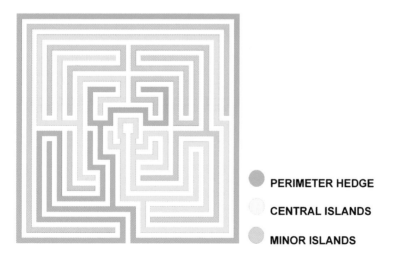

● PERIMETER HEDGE

CENTRAL ISLANDS

● MINOR ISLANDS

The hedge maze at Chevening, Kent, was designed by Earl Stanhope and demonstrates the innovative use of islands of hedges, one of which contains the goal. This increases the difficulty of the maze.

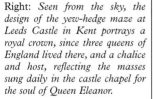

The grotto beneath the hedge maze at Leeds Castle, Kent, is one of the most remarkable grottoes created in the twentieth century. Water cascades over a giant's face in the style of carvings at Bomarzo, Italy. Niches contain female statues representing the four seasons.

Right: *Seen from the sky, the design of the yew-hedge maze at Leeds Castle in Kent portrays a royal crown, since three queens of England lived there, and a chalice and host, reflecting the masses sung daily in the castle chapel for the soul of Queen Eleanor.*

Manor, near Enfield, Middlesex, represents the Victorian era in its series of garden-history reconstructions. Adrian Fisher's design for this maze was inspired by designs of the mid-Victorian period; it was planted with holly in 1989, with a 'secret garden' containing a raised platform reached by a spiral staircase at its goal.

At Somerleyton Hall in Suffolk, William Andrews Nesfield designed a yew-hedge maze, planted in 1846, with a delightful central knoll and pagoda. Mazes survive from this period at other houses open to the public, but they are often too small or fragile to withstand many visitors. The notable hedge maze at Hatfield House, Hertfordshire, planted in yew in

The Italianate maze at Capel Manor, Middlesex, planted in 1989, captures the spirit of the Italianate style of gardening popular in England during the 1840s.

The hedge maze at Somerleyton Hall, Suffolk, was planted in 1846 and has the widest paths of any hedge maze in Britain.

1840 and designed by Lord Mahon, is thought to have replaced an earlier maze in the private gardens. At Woburn Abbey, Bedfordshire, the small circular maze complete with a central painted pavilion forms part of the private gardens. Neither of these private mazes is open to visitors.

A compact yew-hedge maze was planted by William Waldorf Astor at Hever Castle, Kent, in 1905 as part of his restoration of the castle and gardens. The maze formed part of the newly created Tudor Garden to the east of the castle dedicated to Anne Boleyn, who grew up in the castle. A maze was included because it was known to be a favourite device of the Tudors.

The hedge maze at Hever Castle, Kent, is carefully situated so that its design can be appreciated from the castle battlements. It was planted in 1905 by William Waldorf Astor as part of his project to recapture the Tudor character of the castle, which was the home of Anne Boleyn.

POPULAR LEISURE

Hedge mazes continued to be a popular form of entertainment for the Victorians in many public parks and gardens. William Nesfield was commissioned by Prince Albert to design a maze as part of the Royal Horticultural Society's gardens, now the site of the museums in South Kensington, London, funded by profits from the 1851 Great Exhibition.

There were various 'tea-garden' mazes in Victorian times, including one in the Crystal Palace Park in south London and another at Rosherville Gardens, Gravesend, Kent.

A distinctive Victorian trend was the practice of copying the design of an existing hedge maze rather than commissioning a unique design. The most popular design to be copied was that of the Hampton Court maze, which was replicated at Tatton Park, Cheshire (1890), at Albert Park, Middlesbrough (1894), at Knebworth House, Hertfordshire, and in an oval version at Mentmore Towers, Buckinghamshire (1899). At Castle Bromwich Hall, near Birmingham, the now restored maze is a squared mirror image of the Hampton Court maze, planted in holly and hawthorn during this period. Overseas the design was copied at Colonial Williamsburg in Virginia, United States, and also in Australia. The Chevening design was copied in a Victorian public park at Anerley, Norwood, London, at North Woolwich, London, and at Beauport House near Hastings, East Sussex; none of the three still exists. The laurel maze on one side of a steep valley at Glendurgan near Falmouth, Cornwall, was planted in 1833 by Alfred Fox; its meandering hedge pattern was inspired by the hedge maze originally created at the Sydney Gardens in Bath in the late eighteenth century. The 1886 hornbeam-hedge maze at Worden Park, Leyland, Lancashire, is a copy of the hedge maze at Somerleyton Hall.

CHURCH MAZES

The earliest example of a maze in an English church is a fifteenth-century roof boss in the north aisle of St Mary Redcliffe church in Bristol. Just 8 inches (203 mm) across, it copies the eleven-ring medieval Christian design of the famous pavement labyrinth of Chartres Cathedral in France.

Several pavement labyrinths were installed within Victorian church restoration

The free-flowing design of the hedge maze at Glendurgan House in Cornwall was based on an earlier maze created in the Sydney Gardens, Bath.

This gilded labyrinth roof boss measures only 8 inches (203 mm) in diameter but contains a complete medieval Christian design. One of 1200 roof bosses within St Mary Redcliffe church in Bristol, it can be found in the north aisle.

schemes. Sir George Gilbert Scott built a pavement labyrinth of black and white stone measuring 20 feet (6 metres) square beneath the west tower of Ely Cathedral, Cambridgeshire, in 1870. His design demonstrates that knowledge of internal rotational symmetry had become lost, since it does not conform to this secret hallmark of medieval Christian pavement labyrinths. In Bourn church, Cambridgeshire, a rectangular version of the Hampton Court hedge maze was laid beneath the west tower in red and black tiles in 1875; later a font was placed in the centre of it, rather disrupting the pattern. The Watts Memorial Chapel in Compton, Surrey, uses the labyrinth motif in terracotta on an outdoor decorative frieze to symbolise Christ's statement 'I am the Way, the Truth and the Life'. A tile labyrinth lies on the floor at the east end of the church in Itchen Stoke, Hampshire.

The medieval Christian turf maze at Alkborough, Lincolnshire, was copied by the squire of the village, Mr J. Goulton-Constable, as a pavement labyrinth within the church porch and in stained glass above the altar. When he died in 1922 a further design was included on the cross of his gravestone. In Hadstock, Essex, the gravestone of the renowned sculptor Michael Ayrton (1921–75) features an 18 inch (457 mm) wide bronze replica of the full-size brick labyrinth he built at Arkville, New York State, United States.

The pavement maze beneath the west tower of Ely Cathedral, Cambridgeshire, was laid in 1870. The maze, of black and white stone, is 20 feet (6 metres) square; the total path length is 215 feet (66 metres), the height of the tower.

Modern mazes

The social and economic upheaval of two world wars imposed harsh neglect on existing gardens. For half a century it was difficult to maintain gardens, let alone develop them, and many existing mazes were abandoned while few new ones were created. Since the 1980s, however, there has been a renaissance in maze building in Britain and around the world, and a great number of new mazes have been built. Many of the new generation of mazes are based on elaborate emblematic schemes that link them to their surroundings or local history.

Creating a new maze, from conception, design and construction to the formal opening, can be a compelling experience for the owner. Lady Brunner at Greys Court, Oxfordshire, described the various craftsmen involved as her 'band of brothers' and herself chose the inscriptions on the central pillar; Mrs Veronica Tritton at Parham Park, West Sussex, relived her childhood by placing a maze where she had played on her bicycle as a girl. In some ways creating a maze is like painting a portrait, with the age-old relationship between patron and artist developing between maze owner and designer. The maze designer may start with the owner's ideas, the history of the location, and stories, traditions and aspects of contemporary life; practical matters such as deciding dimensions, specifying materials and designing the puzzle follow later.

Various factors contribute to the modern fascination with mazes. A maze is the ultimate landscape artefact to enter, put oneself into and interact with. The maze invites exploration and wonder and, like all the best games, is astonishingly simple in its concept. It is immensely sociable, offering an experience to share with friends, family members and the other visitors you meet within its bounds. Following a maze involves continual movement, so that one's perspective constantly changes. It is the element of fun, of probing

The design for Veronica's Maze at Parham Park in West Sussex was inspired by the ancient embroidery over the Great Bed within the house. Built in 1991, this was Britain's first one-way puzzle maze.

the puzzle, of a journey of discovery that continues to fascinate. The maze also has advantages over other theme park attractions; visitors can make their own choices and progress at their own pace, and they do not have to queue to join in the fun.

Yet a maze can also convey imagery and symbolism, from the entertaining and frivolous to the sublime, so that the pleasure of solving the physical puzzle is heightened by discovering its secret mysteries. The fantastic Beatles' Maze (no longer existing) with its 18 ton steel Yellow Submarine, at the 1984 Liverpool International Garden Festival, and the contemplative Archbishop's Maze at Greys Court, Oxfordshire, abounding in Christian symbolism, were both entirely appropriate in their different ways.

One of the delights of Britain's mazes is their diversity. Because of the climate and the national enthusiasm for gardens, hedge mazes are particularly characteristic of Britain. The eight surviving ancient turf mazes have been joined by a remarkable variety of modern turf mazes, using paths of brick, stone or gravel instead of the traditional turf to walk on. Pavement mazes have been made both in stone and with various colours of brick. Seasonal mazes created in cornfields each summer out of maize have, since 1993, become a worldwide phenomenon. Mirror mazes have been reinvented and are enjoying a renaissance both in Britain and around the world. New ideas with water mazes are creating excitement. Other modern mazes make use of panels, wood, mosaic, marble and stained glass.

The nature of puzzlement has also developed. Turf mazes have been transformed by the addition of junctions and one-way rules, which make them into puzzle mazes. Their size makes it difficult to work out the whole puzzle at once and, perhaps surprisingly, children tend not to cheat in them. An added refinement in several modern hedge mazes is a quick exit route, so that visitors do not have to wander through the maze again to get out. Sometimes this involves going over or under a bridge, as at Scone Palace in Perth & Kinross and the Alice-in-Wonderland Family Park in Dorset. In the yew-hedge maze at Leeds Castle, Kent, the explorer reaches a high central tower, then goes underground into a decorated grotto with water cascades and spotlit statues in niches and can take a quick exit through a 90 foot (30 metre) long secret tunnel running beneath the hedges. In cornfields, maize mazes are on a scale never previously experienced, typically involving 3 or 4 miles (5 or 6 km) – and, in record-breaking instances, up to 8 miles (13 km) – of paths. Maize mazes have achieved three-dimensional networks of paths of unprecedented complexity, using as many as eight bridges to achieve twenty or more crossovers.

New mazes are being created in zoos, amusement parks and holiday countryside settings. Outdoor pavement mazes bring vitality to courtyards and city centres, whilst indoors there are floor mazes, wall mazes in ceramic tile or mosaic, stained-glass maze windows and mirror mazes.

MODERN HEDGE MAZES
Stately homes provide landscape settings for many impressive new hedge mazes, including the yew maze at Chatsworth House in

Above left: *The design of the beech-hedge maze at Russborough House in County Wicklow, Republic of Ireland, includes a diamond motif, reflecting the Beit family's early involvement in the diamond industry.*

Above right: *The beech-hedge maze at Scone Palace in Perth & Kinross is in the shape of the Murray family's five-pointed star. The rows of intersecting hedges are planted alternately in green and copper beech, thus creating a woven tartan effect.*

Derbyshire, and the beech mazes at Scone Palace, Perth & Kinross, and Russborough House in County Wicklow, Ireland. Hedge mazes have been created larger than ever before, with bridges and other high viewing points proving very popular with visitors. For sheer puzzlement, few compare with the giant three-dimensional maze at Longleat House in Wiltshire; it is Britain's largest hedge maze and can take over an hour to solve, with its various wooden bridges and spiralling hedges creating perpetual disorientation.

The Longleat hedge maze has an abstract design of curves and swirls, and six wooden bridges that create a three-dimensional puzzle. There are no hidden meanings or symbolism; everything in this design is dictated by the aim of confusing visitors.

The Marlborough Maze at Blenheim Palace in Oxfordshire portrays the panoply of victory of the first Duke of Marlborough at the Battle of Blenheim in 1704. The design features a giant firing cannon, pyramids of cannonballs, four trumpets, a flag and a banner. Sir Winston Churchill was born at Blenheim Palace so his 'V' for 'Victory' sign is also included.

Left: *The beech hedges of the Saxon Maze at The Herb Farm in Sonning Common, near Reading, are in the shape of four eighth-century Saxon sea creatures. With their decorative, culinary, medicinal and aromatic properties, herbs played an indispensable part in Saxon life.*

Below: *The Dragon Maze at Newquay Zoo in Cornwall was planted with Elaeagnus bushes, which tolerate salt-laden sea air. Mythical creatures are often feared within labyrinths, but here the beast is the labyrinth itself.*

On this grand scale hedge mazes provide superb opportunities for conveying imagery and symbolism. The Marlborough Maze at Blenheim Palace in Oxfordshire portrays the panoply of victory at the Battle of Blenheim and was inspired by Grinling Gibbons's decorative stone carvings on the roof of the palace. The lines of the hedges form images of trumpets, banners, cannonballs and a giant cannon, and the maze incorporates high wooden bridges and brick and stone pavilions.

The Saxon Maze at The Herb Farm in Sonning Common, near Reading, derives its hedge design from Saxon sea creatures illustrated in an eighth-century manuscript; the eyes of the creatures are planted with herbs. The maze is surrounded by an earth rampart and approached over water. At Newquay Zoo in Cornwall the labyrinth itself is a mythical beast, since the sinuous hedges form the coils of a dragon.

The beech-hedge maze at the Alice-in-Wonderland Family Park near Bournemouth, Dorset, features various characters from the famous Alice story by Lewis Carroll.

The centrepiece of the Alice-in-Wonderland Family Park in Dorset is a giant octagonal beech maze 240 feet (73 metres) across. The design includes outline figures of Alice, the Mad Hatter, the Dodo and other characters from *Alice's Adventures in Wonderland*.

The spirit of earlier ages continues to be recreated in various ways. The Jubilee Maze at Symonds Yat, Herefordshire, was inspired by the concept of the Labyrinth of Love of the late fifteenth and sixteenth centuries; it is relatively simple in design and has a temple at the centre and a raised viewing platform from which to admire the maze after solving it.

The renewed interest in historical gardens since the 1980s has led to some exciting and ambitious restoration schemes. Documentary and oral sources, combined with new archaeological techniques developed specifically to investigate abandoned gardens, have enabled accurate restorations to be made of several Victorian hedge mazes. These include mazes at Bridge End Gardens at Saffron Walden in Essex, Rhinefield House in Hampshire, Castle Bromwich Hall Gardens near Birmingham, Saltwell Park in Gateshead and Crystal Palace Park in south London.

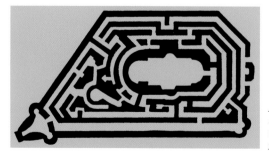

A plan of the Bridge End Gardens maze, Saffron Walden, Essex, created in 1839 and replanted in 1984 as part of the restoration programme for the gardens.

When seen from the sky, the upright wooden logs of the Bicton Park Maze in Devon portray a footprint that would belong to a giant the height of the Eiffel Tower.

PANEL MAZES

Mazes of wooden fence panels can be built and installed within a few weeks. The wooden maze at Holywell Bay Fun Park near Newquay in Cornwall is on a windy cliff top where few bushes could survive; it has a walk-through parting waterfall, foaming fountain gates, bridges, movable panels and a central tower. There are also wooden mazes at Bicton Park in Devon and at Robin Hill Country Park on the Isle of Wight.

The Multi-Sensory Mobility Maze for the Blind was built in 1993 at New College in Worcester, Britain's foremost secondary school for the blind. The maze provides a safe training environment in which to practise moving around in a confusing and dangerous world. For maximum variety the maze has twenty-eight kinds of vertical barriers and path surfaces, as well as changes in level, bridges, a spiral staircase, a tower and water features.

The Maze for the Blind at New College, Worcester, contains statues and sculpture, a telephone kiosk, a post-box, a fully functioning pelican crossing and one and a half cars. Sections of brick wall have gaps that a blind child can learn to detect without touching – by listening, and by sensing the changes of air pressure on his or her face.

MIRROR MAZES

A mirror maze offers a different character of maze experience. The challenge in finding your way through a mirror maze lies less in the complicated layout and more in the illusions and deceptions of the mirrors. The eye is tricked and the brain deceived, and a mirror maze typically seems six times larger than it really is.

Mirror mazes were created at Blackpool Pleasure Beach and Southport Pleasure Beach in the mid twentieth century, with pillars about 4 feet (1.2 metres) apart. A similar scale was used in the 1980s for the Techniquest Science Centre in Cardiff. A mirror maze was opened in 2003 in the Hokus Pokus Gothic mansion at Chessington World of Adventures, Surrey.

In the 1990s a new generation of mirror mazes was pioneered in Britain with larger width between pillars, thus achieving a greater sense of space. Since visitors cannot touch the mirrors on both sides at once there is a heightened sense of disorientation. The Magical Mirror Maze was created at Wookey Hole Caves, Somerset, in 1991; its playful character is achieved through its design, colour scheme, lighting and choice of soundtrack.

In King Arthur's Mirror Maze at Longleat House, Wiltshire, visitors are invited to imagine

The Magical Mirror Maze at Wookey Hole Caves, Somerset, was created in 1991 to celebrate the Year of the Maze. It gives the illusion of spacious avenues of pillars in all directions, rather like a giant colonnade.

King Arthur's Mirror Maze at Longleat House in Wiltshire, in which visitors play the part of knights of the Round Table. The first episode of their journey is through an enchanted forest, where they may glimpse the sword in the stone.

they are knights of the Round Table, performing a quest. This is the world's first mirror maze with two episodes – an enchanted forest and a ruined chapel. In the forest, knights encounter the sword in the stone, which mysteriously appears and rises before disappearing from sight; the mirrors are arranged to achieve a scattered forest-like feel. Within the chapel, visitors find a stained-glass window, the Round Table and a manifestation of the chalice of the Holy Grail, which appears and disappears from sight. A fully three-dimensional effect has been created throughout this maze with its trees, foliage and vaulted stonework.

The second episode in King Arthur's Mirror Maze at Longleat is a ruined chapel, where visitors find the Round Table, a stained-glass window, and perhaps catch sight of the Holy Grail. This was the world's first mirror maze with two episodes.

Cornfield mazes allow design creativity on an unprecedented scale. The three-dimensional illusion produced by this giant image of a castle, created at Belvedere Plantation in Virginia, United States, deceives the eye with its use of perspective. In fact this entire 8 acre (3 hectare) design, with 4 miles (6 km) of paths, was constructed in a level cornfield.

MAIZE MAZES

Maize mazes offer visitors a taste of the living countryside: a puzzling challenge to be solved within a working cornfield. For farmers such mazes provide a welcome form of farm diversification to supplement other forms of income. Since maize corn is a seasonal crop the puzzle maze exists for only a few weeks before being harvested and fed to cattle. Every year there is a new design in the same cornfield, which encourages repeat visits. Adrian Fisher designed the world's first maize maze in Pennsylvania, United States, in 1993 and creates some fifty maize mazes each year around the world. During the summer of 2003 there were forty maize mazes in Britain, open between mid July and mid September.

The Windmill Maize Maze at Millets Farm, Oxfordshire, in 1996 set a new world record for the largest maze in the world, as recognised by the 'Guinness Book of World Records'. The design covered 8 acres (3 hectares) with 4 miles (6 km) of paths.

Above: *Tulleys Farm, West Sussex, has had a different maize maze design each year since 1998, when it started with this playful Dragon Maize Maze.*

Right: *This maize maze portraying a pirate galleon at Tulleys Farm, West Sussex, reached a worldwide audience when it appeared on the CNN website as 'Photo of the Day' in July 1999.*

Below: *The 2000 maize maze at Tulleys Farm, West Sussex, depicted a castle flying on a cloud. It was the world's first maize maze to include a Y-shaped bridge.*

Farmers often use great imagination and creativity in their maize mazes. In 1999 at Millets Farm, Oxfordshire, the central goal of the Pirate Maze contained tons of sand, palm trees and a beached raft.

Cornfield mazes allow great creativity in offering mazes to the public, with complex bridges to achieve remarkable three-dimensional networks, themes, costumes and soundtracks to convey the storyline, and courtyard activities ranging from six-minute mazes to petting zoos, pedal karts and hay-wagon rides. One year a pirate storyline inspired a 'treasure island' made of tons of sand and palm trees within a cornfield; another year a jungle-escape theme was heightened by having a wrecked aircraft among the cornstalks to set visitors on their way. In the United States many cornfield mazes continue until the end of October and towards the end of their season include Hallowe'en activities.

WATER MAZES

The very idea of using water with mazes creates excitement. Together they combine the sparkling light, movement and freshness of water with the physical and mental challenge of the maze. Although there are relatively few examples, water has been used in remarkably diverse ways in British mazes.

Britain's most exciting water maze is on the island of Jersey in the Channel Islands. By day it provides endless fun for visitors to the adjacent sandy beach; by night vertical lights pick out its ever-changing patterns of fountains to reveal a stunning yet sophisticated display. The walls of fountain jets rise and fall, so that sometimes there is an open gap between two cells and

Families get a taste of the living countryside when they explore a cornfield maize maze. Maize grows at a remarkable 1 inch (25 mm) per day, and in Britain forms a barrier above head height by the end of July each year.

The Jersey Water Maze in St Helier is an entertaining sea-front attraction on the Channel Island of Jersey. The walls consist of 208 water jets that change their configuration from moment to moment, thus giving the maze the additional dimension of time.

By night, the Jersey Water Maze provides a sophisticated night-life display of water and light.

sometimes not. The puzzle route through the maze is in a constant state of change.

The Beatles' Maze at the 1984 Liverpool International Garden Festival also incorporated water, but here it was used as the barrier between the raised brick paths; the whole concept was that of a

The Beatles' Maze was one of the most popular features of the 1984 International Garden Festival in Liverpool. The maze paths consisted of clay-brick pavers set in a giant apple-shaped pool, leading to the conning-tower of a 51 feet (16 metres) long, 18 ton Yellow Submarine. The maze was opened by Her Majesty Queen Elizabeth II and won two gold medals and one of the top ten festival awards.

psychedelic garden, with stepping-stones in the shape of musical notes and with a ring of apple trees planted around the maze. A million people walked through the Beatles' Maze during the six months of the festival. Afterwards, the maze's 51 feet (16 metres) long Yellow Submarine was relocated to central Liverpool, close to the Liver Building.

At Legoland near Windsor, Britain's most spectacular walk-through parting waterfall guards the entrance to the Tudor Hedge Maze. This water feature within mazes, along with foaming fountain gates, was pioneered by Adrian Fisher. A parting waterfall needs a vertical edifice from which to flow – in this case a wall with castellated turrets; it needs a sizeable pool into which to fall; and, the pool being an obstacle, it requires a footbridge over which to cross the pool. Once across, visitors find the waterfall blocking the bridge. This absurd and contrived problem has an ingenious solution: as you cross the bridge at walking speed the waterfall magically parts and allows you to enter the maze without getting wet. Legoland and its three mazes were opened in 1996.

The maze path of the Bristol Water Maze in Victoria Park, Bristol, is a water channel running between barriers of brick and is primarily to be looked at rather than walked along. Its design is a copy of the medieval Christian roof-boss maze at the nearby St Mary Redcliffe church, which cuts the horizon, and towards which this water maze is aligned.

The Tudor Hedge Maze at Legoland, Windsor, can be entered only after passing through a waterfall. The waterfall parts automatically as visitors approach, thus providing them with a dry way through.

The course of the Bristol Water Maze in Victoria Park, Bristol, is not a path but a brick channel. Water wells up at the centre and follows the structure's eleven rings. The maze is aligned with the spire of St Mary Redcliffe church on the horizon a mile away and was inspired by the roof-boss maze in that church's north aisle.

Hever Castle in Kent has a modern water maze, with paths of paving stones set within a large pool. Fine water jets provide additional barriers. The goal is a central grotto with steps leading up to a tower viewpoint above.

One of Britain's most distinctive labyrinthine experiences is not a formal maze. Opened in 1996, the Forbidden Corner near Leyburn in North Yorkshire covers 4 acres (2 hectares) with a myriad of riddles, visual illusions and surprises. It contains a 'temple of the underworld', a pyramid of translucent glass, a ruined castle and a hedgerow maze. A stone chasm leads into a series of underground chambers; one room has six identical doors and a floor that slowly revolves, leaving you unsure of which way you came in and which way leads out. In various places hidden nozzles squirt visitors with thin jets of water.

The modern water maze at Hever Castle in Kent lies within a large pool and has a central tower with a grotto beneath. Fine water jets across the paths add to the entertainment.

The Tudor Rose Maze at Kentwell Hall, Suffolk, was created in 1985 to mark the five-hundredth anniversary of the accession of the Tudor dynasty.

PAVEMENT MAZES

The Tudor Rose Maze fills the courtyard of Kentwell Hall in Suffolk, and windows at every level look out on to the design. Made of twenty-six thousand paving bricks in different colours, it can be enjoyed either as a puzzle maze or as five separate unicursal mazes. Its fifteen diamonds contain incised brick images relating to the Tudor dynasty, while the centre forms a giant chessboard.

The pedestrianised town centre at Worksop in Nottinghamshire has a brick pavement maze at each end, each having a heraldic theme – a Lion Rampant and a Unicorn Rampant. Using four colours of brickwork, the maze paths weave in and out of the bodies of these giant creatures

Below: The Unicorn Rampant and Lion Rampant mazes in Worksop town centre, Nottinghamshire, are pavement mazes portraying the Royal Family's coat of arms. Visitors enter at the foot, and the goal is each creature's head; the maze paths, partly within the body and partly outside, run between the darker lines of the design.

A giant stag beetle chases an ant across the four pavement mazes at Abbotswood Shopping Centre, Yate, Gloucestershire. This ingenious paving combines circular rings of brick with the rectangular patterns of the central mazes.

before finally reaching the goal of either the lion's crown or the unicorn's horn. The design of four pavement mazes at the Abbotswood Shopping Centre in Yate, Gloucestershire, is invaded by a huge stag beetle and a giant ant. At Edinburgh Zoo an orang-utan portrayed in seven-sided paving bricks patented by Adrian Fisher lies at the centre of the Darwin hedge maze. The pavement maze at

Above: *This 20 by 20 foot (6 by 6 metre) pavement maze lies at the goal of the Darwin Maze at Edinburgh Zoo. Laid in seven-sided pavers, it portrays an orang-utan sitting on a high branch in the rainforest; in the background, Man has set fire to the rainforest. Thus the creature risks extinction through the destruction of its habitat.*

The Darwin Maze at Edinburgh Zoo helps visitors to find out about the theory of evolution. The maze has been designed in the shape of a Galapagos tortoise to reflect the fact that Charles Darwin first came up with his theory while in the Galapagos Islands.

The pavement maze at Shawford Parish Hall near Winchester marks the nine-hundredth anniversary of the death of King William Rufus in 1100. The design uses vibrant seven-sided Fisher Pavers to portray the events surrounding the king's death while hunting deer in the New Forest.

Shawford Parish Hall near Winchester was dedicated in 2000 to mark the nine-hundredth anniversary of the death of King William Rufus in the New Forest on 3rd August 1100.

Mazes have a strong educational and 'discovery' value and have appeared in many schools and their playgrounds. Notable examples of school mazes using decorative paving include Cliff School, Wakefield, which has an oval colour maze and a smaller square maze; Elson Junior School, Hampshire, with two mazes and distinctive random basket-weave paving; St John's School, Moordown, Bournemouth, with the school's Lamb of God emblem; St John's College School, Cambridge, with a maze and a giant spider's web; New Milton Junior School, Hampshire, with four pavement mazes, each having different rules to follow; and Mary Hare School for the Deaf near Newbury, Berkshire, with a spiral scheme filling the sixth-form courtyard.

The colour maze principle is used in the brick pavement maze in front of the Mathematics Building at Leicester University. Here the junction squares are connected by paths of different colours, and each time one reaches a

The maze courtyard at St John's Primary School, Moordown, Bournemouth, portrays the school's motif of the Pascal Lamb. By rotating the paving by 45 degrees, the resulting 'square' is larger than the width of the courtyard. The author is a former pupil of the school.

The playground at New Milton Junior School in Hampshire contains four pavement mazes, each with a different rule to follow.

node one must leave on a path of a different colour; the object, as with all mazes, is to reach the goal. In some colour mazes one can change to any other path colour; in this instance one must follow a three-colour sequence repeatedly.

PATH-IN-GRASS MAZES

Traditional turf mazes are nowadays impractical, since their turf paths cannot withstand the wear and tear of large numbers of visitors. To overcome this, several modern turf mazes have paths of hard paving, yet grass remains the dominant feature, being used as the barrier between the paths.

The Archbishop's Maze at Greys Court, Oxfordshire, dedicated

The Archbishop's Maze at Greys Court in Oxfordshire is a modern interpretation of a Christian turf maze and abounds in Christian symbolism. The brick paths set in grass lead to a simple Roman cross of Bath stone, superimposed within an elaborate Byzantine cross of blue Westmorland stone. These superimposed crosses symbolise the reconciliation of East and West, both in religious and in contemporary political terms.

by the then Archbishop of Canterbury, Dr Robert Runcie, in 1981, consists of brick paths winding between wide strips of turf. It was conceived by Lady Brunner in response to a passage in the address Dr Runcie made at his enthronement in which he described a dream he had had about a maze whose pattern was clear to those who stood outside it but puzzling to those who 'fretted and fumed inside'. The maze is full of Christian symbolism, with a Latin cross and a Byzantine cross superimposed at its centre to proclaim the reconciliation of East and West.

Nearby, along the banks of the Thames, lie two other brick path-in-grass mazes, at Marlow and Windsor. Both use the one-way puzzle rule – that once you have started you must always keep going forwards. Using symbolic path patterns and four mosaic sections, the Millennium Maze in Higginson Park, Marlow, celebrates the history of Marlow from the Vikings that sailed up the Thames a thousand years ago to the rowing achievements in the 2000 Olympics of Sir Steve Redgrave, Marlow's most famous living resident. The Royal Windsor Maze takes its inspiration from the arrival of the railways in Windsor during Queen Victoria's reign. The various maze paths have points and curves and run through low 'cuttings'; there is also paving depicting each of the chess pieces using seven-sided Fisher Pavers, and finally an image of the Round Tower of Windsor Castle.

In the Water Tower Gardens in Chester, three maze networks of different colours share the same layout of paths; each maze is a separate one-way challenge, passing through nine intricate junction squares. The total effect can be seen from the overlooking Roman city walls, with dramatic triple-striped paths curving and intersecting, and not a straight path in the entire design.

The elegant spiralling brick maze at Parham Park in West Sussex echoes intricate Elizabethan needlework displayed within the house and is also a baffling one-way puzzle maze in that one must keep going forwards once one has started.

By contrast, railway engines provide inspiration for path mazes at the Lappa Valley Railway in Cornwall and near Newcastle upon Tyne, respectively portraying Richard Trevithick's tramroad locomotive and George Stephenson's *Rocket*.

The paths of the Bath Festival Maze, Somerset, are appropriately made in local Bath stone, contrasting vividly with the darker grass barriers. Seating is provided by three sections of low stone walls around the maze.

The Millennium Maze in Higginson Park, Marlow, Buckinghamshire, has a one-way maze logic. Its main design depicts eleven fish in a feeding frenzy, and it has four 'mitre' mosaics depicting the town's history, including Sir Steve Redgrave's gold medals for rowing in the 2000 Olympics.

'The Maze' was the chosen theme of the 1984 Bath International Music Festival. Few of the festival's themes have seen such a tangible manifestation as this – an elliptical path maze set in grass beside the River Avon. The domed centrepiece, 15 feet (4.5 metres) in diameter, contains seventy-two thousand pieces of mosaic, portraying seven aspects of the city of Bath.

MOSAIC MAZES

The centrepiece of the Bath Festival Maze is a giant mosaic of seventy-two thousand pieces of Italian tesserae, 15 feet (4.5 metres) in diameter, portraying the famous Gorgon's head and other aspects of Bath's Celtic and Roman past. Each of seven mosaic panels forms a 'gaze maze', which can be followed and solved by eye, and this provides a fascinating reward for reaching the centre.

On a smaller scale, the wall mosaic maze at Wyck Rissington church in Gloucestershire is set at a low level so that children can trace it with their fingers; it is in memory of Canon Harry Cheales, a former rector of the parish, who built a full-size maze to the same design in the rectory garden after having a vivid dream.

The Sun Maze at Longleat in Wiltshire had a giant mosaic installed in 2003 to form its centrepiece under a shallow pool of water; its design shimmers with the slightest rippling, to the great delight of anyone viewing it from the upper windows of Longleat House.

The centrepiece of the Bath Festival Maze is a giant domed mosaic consisting of seven 'gaze mazes'. Each is a separate maze, to be traced by the eye. The dolphin mosaic maze has paths of white mosaic tesserae, to be followed from one tail to the other.

In a 'maths maze', one can start on any square and the challenge is to reach the central square with a running score of zero. Each time one moves, add or subtract from the running total. After solving this maze no one can claim an inability to do mental arithmetic!

HUMAN-SCALE PUZZLES

The public fascination with human-scale and 'hands-on' puzzles has grown. Many modern puzzles have a strong element of discovery and also have maze-like chains of logic in their functioning. This serves to encourage logical and lateral thinking, as well as to develop the memorising of long chains of consecutive moves.

Maze and puzzle festivals lasting between a week and a month have proved immensely popular at historic properties including Hampton Court Palace, Leeds Castle and Polesden Lacey, as well as at retail destinations

In a 'colour maze', one has to switch to a path of a different colour at each decision point. The precise rules can vary from design to design; sometimes one must alternate between two colours, or follow a strict colour sequence, and sometimes one is allowed to change to any other colour. The same colour-maze design can be laid in brick paving in school playgrounds or appear as a portable maze in bright plastic tiles.

In an 'arrow maze', each square offers one a change of direction – but one chooses the distance to jump. The maze paths are invisible hops through the air.

Below: *'Rolling-block mazes' are unusual in that it is an object, not a person, that does the moving. Doing such a maze involves rolling a block around a layout similar to a crossword puzzle, always staying off the black squares. Like regular mazes, these puzzles have a distinct network of choices and dead-ends.*

Above: *'Finger mazes' satisfy every child's desire to touch and feel, and to run their fingers along a groove. There are numerous variations, including single-sided and double-sided finger mazes and those with one-way rules. Their repeat popularity makes them especially suitable for schools.*

This inflatable maze at Gunwharf Quays, Portsmouth, is one of the dozens of mazes and puzzles set up during the August 'Maze Month' festival.

such as Gunwharf Quays in Portsmouth. These events have featured numerous six-minute mazes, including rolling block mazes, plastic tile floor mazes, inflatable mazes, rope mazes, finger mazes, tilting mazes, jigtile puzzles and other portable mazes.

A permanent Maze and Puzzle Garden was created at Staunton Country Park to commemorate the Queen's Golden Jubilee in 2002. One enters into a puzzle garden, with different spaces and hollows containing different full-scale puzzles and challenges; the climax is a yew-hedge maze with wrought-iron maze gates portraying the lion and the unicorn, an amusing mouth-and-ear speaking tube, and decorative paving that indicates the available path choices beneath each of five wrought-iron arbours.

The diversity of Britain's mazes is unparalleled anywhere in the world and continues to develop with new and delightful creations. Let us hope that Britain's mazes and labyrinths will entertain and fascinate visitors for many generations to come.

One of a pair of wrought-iron maze gates within the Golden Jubilee Maze at Staunton Country Park, Hampshire, portraying the royal beasts, the lion and the unicorn. Each maze gate has an intriguing maze to follow with one's finger.

Further reading and organisations

BOOKS

Fisher, Adrian. *Mind Bending Maze Puzzles*. Lagoon Books, 1999. A collection of mazes with rules compiled by Adrian Fisher.

Fisher, Adrian. *Mazes and Follies*. Jarrold Publishing, 2004. Some of the quirkiest and most beautiful features of the English landscape.

Fisher, Adrian, and Gerster, Georg. *The Art of the Maze*. Weidenfeld & Nicolson, 1990. The modern definitive work on mazes worldwide, with over a hundred colour illustrations.

Fisher, Adrian, and Loxton, Howard. *Secrets of the Maze*. Thames & Hudson (United Kingdom), Barrons Educational, New York (United States), 1998. An interactive guide to the world's most amazing mazes.

Fisher, Adrian, and Saward, Jeff. *The British Maze Guide*. Adrian Fisher Mazes Limited, 1991.

Kraft, John. *The Goddess in the Labyrinth*. Abo Akaderni, 1985.

Matthews, W. H. *Mazes and Labyrinths – Their History and Development*. 1922; reprinted by Dover, New York, 1970. The definitive work on mazes, though inevitably deficient on the twentieth century.

Pennick, Nigel. *Mazes and Labyrinths*. Robert Hale, 1990. Places mazes and labyrinths in their historical context.

Saward, Jeff. *Magical Paths*. Mitchell Beazley, 2002.

Saward, Jeff. *Labyrinths and Mazes*. Gaia Books, 2003.

ORGANISATIONS

Adrian Fisher Mazes Limited, Portman Lodge, Durweston, Dorset DT11 0QA. Telephone: 01258 458845. Email: sales@mazemaker.com Websites: www.mazemaker.com, www.mirrormaze.com, www.maizemaze.com, www.pavingmaze.com and www.sixminutemazes.com (The world's leading maze company; see below for further information.)

Caerdroia, 53 Thundersley Grove, Thundersley, Benfleet, Essex SS7 3EB. Telephone: 01268 751915. Email: info@labyrinthos.net Website: www.labyrinthos.net (Its magazine, *Caerdroia*, has been regularly published by Jeff Saward since 1980.)

Mazes created by Adrian Fisher Mazes Limited

Adrian Fisher Mazes Limited (before 1986, Minotaur Designs) was involved in the design of the following mazes and labyrinths within the British Isles, as well as over three hundred other projects in twenty-three countries. This list does not include cornfield maize mazes (see www.maizemaze.com), maze events or mazes installed in private gardens. Mazes within school grounds are not open to the general public.

Hedge mazes: Alice-in-Wonderland Family Park, Dorset; Alnwick Water Gardens, Northumberland; Blackpool Pleasure Beach, Lancashire; Blenheim Palace, Oxfordshire; Capel Manor, Middlesex; Dobbies Gardenworld, Atherstone, Warwickshire; Edinburgh Zoo; Escot Park, Devon; The Herb Farm at Sonning Common, near Reading, Berkshire; Leeds Castle, Kent; Legoland, Windsor, Berkshire; Newquay Zoo, Cornwall; Portman Lodge, Dorset (private); Russborough House, County Wicklow; Scone Palace, Perth & Kinross; Staunton Country Park, Hampshire.

The entrance of the Chinese Dragon Maze at Blackpool Pleasure Beach is guarded by two bronze dragons, whose water jets cut out as one approaches – only to surprise one afresh with a burst of fog when one is on the bridge.

Mirror mazes: Absolut Vodka Mirror Maze, Oxo Gallery, London (2002 only); King Arthur's Mirror Maze, Longleat House, Wiltshire; Wookey Hole Caves, Somerset.

Mosaic mazes: central mosaic of the Bath Festival Maze, Beazer Gardens, Bath, Somerset; Wyck Rissington church, Gloucestershire.

Path-in-grass mazes: Archbishop's Maze, Greys Court, Oxfordshire; Bath Festival Maze, Beazer Gardens, Bath, Somerset; Goswells Park, Windsor, Berkshire; Higginson Park, Marlow, Buckinghamshire; Lappa Valley Railway, Cornwall; Parham Park, West Sussex; Portman Lodge, Dorset (private); Water Tower Gardens, Chester, Cheshire.

Paving mazes: Alton Junior School, Hampshire; Cliff School, Wakefield, West Yorkshire; County Mall, Crawley, West Sussex; Elson Junior School, Hampshire; Leicester University; Lion Rampant Maze and Unicorn Rampant Maze, Worksop, Nottinghamshire; Mary Hare School for the Deaf, Newbury, Berkshire; New Milton Junior School, Hampshire; Orang-utan Pavement Maze, Darwin Maze, Edinburgh Zoo; St John's College School, Cambridge; St John's School, Moordown, Dorset; Shawford Parish Hall, Hampshire; Sydney Russell School, Dagenham, Essex; Tudor Rose Maze, Kentwell Hall, Suffolk; Westfield School, East Sussex.

Six-minute mazes: Alice-in-Wonderland Family Park, Dorset; Blackpool Zoo, Lancashire; Blenheim Palace, Oxfordshire; Flambards Theme Park, Cornwall; Holker Hall, Cumbria; Mugdock Park, Glasgow; Staunton Country Park, Hampshire.

Water mazes: Beatles' Maze, Liverpool International Garden Festival (1984 only); Jersey Water Maze, St Helier, Jersey.

Wooden mazes: Bicton Park, Devon; Holywell Bay Fun Park, Cornwall; Legoland, Windsor, Berkshire; RNIB New College, Worcester (not open to the public).

Mazes to visit

This is a list of mazes and labyrinths of all kinds that are accessible to the public in the United Kingdom and the Republic of Ireland. However, new mazes are being created every year and occasionally an existing maze ceases to be open to the public; this is particularly true of seasonal maize mazes. Many mazes are at historic houses, gardens or other tourist attractions and intending visitors are advised to find out the opening times before making a special journey. The National Grid Reference (NGR) is given for certain hard-to-find sites. Please respect the owner's privacy for any mazes or labyrinths in private gardens and school playgrounds.

CHANNEL ISLANDS
Jersey
a'Maizin Maze, St Peter. Telephone: 01534 482116. Website: www.jerseymaze.com (Seasonal maize maze.)

Jersey Water Maze, Jardins de la Mer, St Helier. (Water maze with 208 fountain jets, illuminated at night.)

ENGLAND
Berkshire
The Herb Farm, Sonning Common, near Reading RG4 9NJ. Telephone: 0118 972 4220. Website: www.herbfarm.co.uk (The Saxon Maze, hedge maze.)

Legoland, Windsor Park Limited, Winkfield Road, Windsor SL4 4AY. Telephone: 08705 040404. Website: www.lego.com/legoland (Tudor hedge maze with parting waterfall, Celtic maze and nautical maze.)

Buckinghamshire
Chenies Manor House, Chenies, near Rickmansworth WD3 6ER. Telephone: 01494 762888. (Gravel path-in-grass maze; also Chenies Hedge Maze, winner of the *Sunday Times* maze-design competition, created in 1991.)

Willen Lake, Milton Keynes. (Gravel path-in-grass maze.)

Cambridgeshire
Church of St Helen and St Mary, Bourn, near Cambridge. (Pavement maze.)

The Common, Hilton, near Huntingdon. NGR: TL 293663. (Turf maze.)

Ely Cathedral. Website: www.cathedral.ely.anglican.org (Pavement maze.)

Cheshire
Brimstage Hall Maize Maze, Brimstage, Wirral. Telephone: 07919 674977. Website: www.brimstagehall.co.uk (Seasonal maize maze.)

Parkfield, Warrington. (Gravel path-in-grass maze.)

Redhouse Farm Maize Maze, Altrincham. Telephone: 0161 941 3480. Website: www.redhousefarm.co.uk (Seasonal maize maze.)

Tatton Park, Knutsford WA16 6QN. National Trust. Telephone: 01625 534400 or 01625 534435 (infoline). Website: www.tattonpark.org.uk (Hedge maze.)

Cornwall
Glendurgan Garden, Mawnan Smith, near Falmouth TR11 5JZ. National Trust. Telephone: 01326 250906. Website: www.nationaltrust.org.uk (Hedge maze.)

Holywell Bay Fun Park, Holywell Bay, Newquay TR8 5PW. Telephone: 01637 830095. Website: www.holywellbay.co.uk (Wooden fencing maze with bridges, parting waterfall and fountain gates.)

Merlin's Magical Maze at Holywell Bay in Cornwall has bridges, foaming fountain gates and a central tower, and is entered through a walk-through parting waterfall.

Lappa Valley Steam Railway and Leisure Park, St Newlyn East, Newquay TR8 5HZ. Telephone: 01872 510317. Website: www.lappavalley.co.uk (Brick path-in-grass maze.)
Newquay Zoo, Trenance Gardens, Newquay TR7 2TW. Telephone: 01637 873342. Website: www.newquayzoo.co.uk (Dragon maze.)
Padstow Maize Maze, Trevisker Farm, Padstow PL28 8LD. Telephone: 07973 364572. Website: www.maizemaze.com (Seasonal maize maze.)
Rocky Valley, near Tintagel. (Rock carvings.)
St Agnes, Scilly Isles. NGR: SV 876078, 878078. (Stone labyrinths.)
St Martin's, Scilly Isles. NGR: SV 923170. (Stone labyrinths.)
Trenhayle Adventure Park and Maize Maze, Hayle. Website: www.maizemaze.com Telephone: 01736 755631. Email: trenhayle@aol.com (Seasonal maize maze.)

Cumbria
Holker Hall and Gardens, Cark-in-Cartmel, Grange-over-Sands LA11 7PL. Telephone: 01539 558328. Website: www.holker-hall.co.uk (Children's colour mazes.)

Derbyshire
Chatsworth House, Chatsworth, Bakewell DE45 1PP. Telephone: 01246 565300. Website: www.chatsworth.org (Hedge maze.)
Heights of Abraham Country Park, Matlock Bath. Website: www.heights-of-abraham.co.uk (Children's colour maze.)

Devon
Bicton Park, East Budleigh, Budleigh Salterton EX9 7BJ. Telephone: 01395 568465. Website: www.bictongardens.co.uk (Wooden-walled maze.)
South Devon Railway, The Station, Buckfastleigh TQ11 0DZ. Telephone: 01364 642338. Website: www.southdevonrailway.org (Hedge maze.)

Dorset
Alice-in-Wonderland Family Park, Merritown Lane, Hurn, Christchurch. Telephone: 01202 483444. Website: www.aliceinwonderlandpark.co.uk (Alice in Wonderland Maze, hedge maze.)

The Great Dorset Maze, Rodden Farm, near Weymouth, Dorset DT3 4JE. Telephone: 01305 871281. Website: www.greatdorsetmaizemaze.com (Seasonal maize maze.)

Portman Lodge, Durweston, Dorset DT11 0QA. Telephone: 01258 458845. (Hedge maze, turf maze, etc; private.)

Stewart's Garden Lands Maize Maze, Christchurch, Dorset BH23 4SA. Telephone: 01425 272244. Website: www.dorsetmaze.com (Seasonal maize maze.)

Durham

Broom House Farm Maize Maze, near Witton Gilbert. Telephone: 0191 371 9697. Website: www.broomhousedurham.co.uk

Saltwell Park, Gateshead. Website: www.gateshead.gov.uk/saltwellpark (Hedge maze that can be viewed from above but not walked in.)

Essex

Bridge End Gardens, Saffron Walden. Telephone (tourist information centre): 01799 510444. (Hedge maze.)

The Stag Maize Maze at Stewarts Garden Lands in Christchurch, Dorset, in 2002 set a Guinness world record, covering 16 acres (6 hectares) with 8 miles (13 km) of paths.

Below: *The Lobster Maize Maze at Stewarts Garden Lands in 2003 set a further Guinness world record, covering 19 acres (8 hectares) with nearly 9 miles (14 km) of paths. Three different path networks – silver, gold and platinum – provided visitors with increasingly complex challenges.*

The Common, Saffron Walden. NGR: TL 543385. Telephone (tourist information centre): 01799 510444. (Has bricks set into a turf maze, the largest example of this type of maze in the world.)
The Maize Maze at Blake Hall, Ongar. Telephone: 01277 362502. Website: www.blakehall.co.uk
Mistley Place Park, Manningtree CO11 1ER. Telephone: 01206 396483. (Hedge maze.)
Mole Hall Wildlife Park, near Saffron Walden, Essex CB11 3SS. Telephone: 01799 540400. Website: www.molehall.co.uk (Water maze.)
St Botolph's churchyard, Hadstock, near Saffron Walden. (Maze on gravestone of Michael Ayrton.)

Gloucestershire and Bristol

Bourton-on-the-Water. Website: www.bourton-on-the-water.co.uk (Hedge maze.)
Hidcote Manor Farm Maize Maze, Hidcote Bartrim, Chipping Campden GL55 6LP. Telephone: 01386 430178. Website: www.hidcotemaze.co.uk (Seasonal maize maze.)
St Lawrence's church, Wyck Rissington, near Stow-on-the-Wold. (Maze of the Mysteries of the Gospels – wall mosaic.)
St Mary Redcliffe church, Bristol. (Roof-boss maze.)
Victoria Park, Bristol. (Water maze.)

The gravestone of the sculptor Michael Ayrton in Hadstock churchyard, Essex, with its miniature bronze replica of the brick labyrinth Ayrton built at Arkville, New York State.

Hampshire

Breamore Countryside Museum, Breamore House, Breamore, Fordingbridge SP6 2BY. Telephone: 01725 512233. Website: www.hants.gov.uk (Great British Maze, brick path-in-grass maze.)
Golden Jubilee Maze, Staunton Country Park, Havant. Telephone: 023 9245 3405. Website: www.hants.gov.uk (Yew-hedge maze and puzzle garden.)
Hampshire Mega-Maze, near Havant. Telephone: 023 9247 2584. Website: www.strawberryfayre.com (Seasonal maize maze.)
Mayflower Park, Southampton. (Concrete-walled maze.)
Miz-maze, Breamore Down. NGR: SU 142203. (Turf maze.)
Miz-maze, St Catherine's Hill, near Winchester. (Turf maze.)
Oak Tree Farm Maize Maze, Little London, near Basingstoke. Telephone: 01256 851277. Website: www.oaktreefarmshop.co.uk
Paultons Park, Ower, near Romsey SO51 6AL. Telephone: 01703 814442. Website: www.paultonspark.co.uk (Hedge maze.)
Rhinefield House Hotel, near Brockenhurst. (Hedge maze.)
St Mary's church, Itchen Stoke, near Winchester. (Pavement maze beneath altar.)
Shawford Parish Hall, Shawford, near Winchester (Brick pavement maze portraying the death in 1100 of King William Rufus; installed in 2000.)

Herefordshire

Amazing Hedge Puzzle, Symonds Yat West, Ross-on-Wye HR9 6DA. Telephone: 01600 890360. Website: www.btinternet.com/~mazes (Hedge maze and museum of mazes.)
Mappa Mundi, Hereford Cathedral. (Maze representing Crete.)

Hertfordshire

Hatfield House, Hatfield AL9 5NQ. Telephone: 01707 287000. Website: www.hatfield-house.co.uk (Low box maze – may be viewed but not walked in.)

The low box maze at Hatfield House, Hertfordshire, provides a striking horizontal counterpart to the vertical architecture of the Old Palace.

Tring, by the parish church. (Zebra-head brick maze.)

Isle of Wight
Barton Manor Gardens, Whippingham, East Cowes PO32 6LB. Telephone: 01983 528989. (Hedge maze.)
Blackgang Chine, near Ventnor PO38 2HN. Telephone: 01983 730052. Website: www.blackgangchine.com (Hedge maze.)
Robin Hill Country Park, Arreton, Newport PO30 2NU. Website: www.robin-hill.com (Wooden panel maze.)

Kent
Hever Castle, Hever, Edenbridge TN8 7NG. Telephone: 01732 865224. Website: www.hevercastle.co.uk (Hedge maze and water maze.)
Leeds Castle, Maidstone ME17 1PL. Telephone: 01622 765400. Website: www.leeds-castle.com (Hedge maze and grotto.)
Marsh Maize Maze, Dymchurch. Telephone: 01797 366180 or 07951 237821. Website: www.marsh-maize-maze.co.uk

Lancashire
Blackpool Pleasure Beach, Blackpool. Telephone: 08704 445566. Website: www.blackpoolpleasurebeach.co.uk (Hedge maze and mirror maze.)
Blackpool Zoo, Blackpool. Telephone: 01253 830830. Website: www.blackpoolzoo.org.uk (Seasonal maize maze.)
Leighton Hall, Carnforth LA5 9ST. Telephone: 01524 734474. Website: www.leightonhall.co.uk (The Caterpillar Maze, gravel path-in-grass maze.)
Worden Park, Leyland. (Hedge maze.)

Leicestershire

Mathematica, Leicester University, Leicester. (Brick-pavement colour maze in front of the Mathematics Building.)

Wistow Maize Maze, near Great Glen LE8 0QF. Telephone: 07884 403889. Website: www.maizemaze.com

Lincolnshire

Church of St John the Baptist, Alkborough, near Scunthorpe. (Stained-glass window maze; stone pavement maze in porch.)

Doddington Hall, Lincoln LN6 4RU. Telephone: 01522 694308. Website: www.doddingtonhall.com (Gravel path-in-grass maze.)

Julian's Bower, Alkborough, near Scunthorpe. NGR: SE 880218. (Turf maze.)

Thornton Abbey Maize Maze, Thornton Abbey. Telephone: 01469 541893. Website: www.theabbotsgarden.com (Seasonal maize maze.)

Willows Farm Maize Maze, near Skegness. Telephone: 07771 696001. Website: www.willowsfarm.co.uk

London and Middlesex

Capel Manor, Bullsmoor Lane, Enfield, Middlesex EN1 4RQ. Telephone: 020 8366 4442. Website: www.capel.gov.uk (Italianate maze, hedge maze.)

Crystal Palace Maze, Crystal Palace Park, London SE19. (Hedge maze.)

Hampton Court Palace, East Molesey, Surrey KT8 9AU. Telephone: 0870 752 7777. Website: www.hrp.org.uk (The world's oldest surviving hedge maze, planted in 1690.)

Warren Street Playground, Whitfield Street, London W1. (Pavement maze.)

Warren Street Underground Station, London W1. (Wall mazes of ceramic tiles.)

Norfolk

Hilgay Maze. Telephone: 01366 385661 or 01366 383437. Website: www.hilgaymaze.co.uk (Seasonal maize maze.)

Priory Maze and Gardens, Cromer Road, Beeston Regis, Sheringham NR26 8SF. Telephone: 01263 822986. Website: www.priorymazegardens.com

Northumberland

Alnwick Water Gardens, Alnwick. Website: www.alnwickgarden.com (Bamboo maze.)

Springfield Park, Forest Hall, near Newcastle upon Tyne. (Rocket Maze, gravel path-in-grass maze.)

Nottinghamshire

Thoresby Mega Maze, Newark. Telephone: 01623 824763. Website: www.thoresby.com (Seasonal maize maze.)

Oxfordshire

Blenheim Palace, Woodstock. Website: www.blenheimpalace.com (Hedge maze. Also the site of Rosamund's Bower, now destroyed, site marked by a well.)

Millets Farm Centre, Abingdon. Telephone: 01865 391086. Website: www.milletsfarmcentre.com (Seasonal maize maze.)

Shropshire

Adventure Maze, Green Fields Farm, Telford. Telephone: 01952 603747. Website: www.farm-deli.com (Seasonal maize maze.)

Somerset

Bath Festival Maze, Beazer Gardens, Bath. (Stone path-in-grass maze, with central mosaic.)

Court Farm Country Park, near Weston-super-Mare. Telephone: 01934 822383. Website: www.courtfarmcountrypark.co.uk (Seasonal maize maze.)
The Great Western Maze, Newton St Loe, Bath. Telephone: 01793 731806. Website: www.maizemaze.com (Seasonal maize maze.)

Surrey
Watts Memorial Chapel, Compton, near Guildford GU3 1DQ. Telephone: 01483 810235. (Corbels and altar decoration, incorporating labyrinths.)

Sussex
County Mall, Crawley. (Two terrazzo paving mazes.)
Parham House and Gardens, Parham Park, Pulborough RH20 4HS. Telephone: 01903 742021. Website: www.parhaminsussex.co.uk (Veronica's Maze, brick path-in-grass maze.)
Tulleys Farm, Turners Hill, near Crawley RH10 4PE. Telephone: 01342 717071. Website: www.tulleysfarm.com (Seasonal maize maze.)

Warwickshire
Castle Bromwich Hall Gardens, Chester Road, Castle Bromwich, Birmingham B36 9BT. Telephone: 0121 749 4100. Website: www.cbhgt.colebridge.net (Holly-hedge maze.)
Dobbies Gardenworld, Atherstone. Telephone: 01827 715511. Website: www.dobbies.com (A varied collection of mazes, themed on six continents.)
Earlswood Maze, near Solihull. Telephone: 01564 702729. Website: www.earlswoodmaze.com (Seasonal maize maze.)

The double puzzle maze in County Mall, Crawley, paradoxically offers two mutually exclusive paths – one white with black barriers and the other black with white barriers. Together the path areas occupy nearly 100 per cent of the paved surface.

Ragley Hall, near Alcester B49 5NJ. Telephone: 01789 762090. Website: www.ragleyhall.com (Concrete-walled maze.)

Wiltshire
Longleat House, Longleat, Warminster BA12 7NW. Telephone: 01985 844400. Website: www.longleat.co.uk (Longleat has five mazes: the world's longest hedge maze in yew; King Arthur's Mirror Maze; Labyrinth of Love; Moon Labyrinth; Sun Maze.)

Yorkshire
Burton Agnes Hall, Burton Agnes, Driffield YO25 4NB. Telephone: 01262 490324. (Hedge maze.)
Eureka Children's Museum, Discovery Road, Halifax HX1 2NE. Telephone: 01422 330069. Website: www.eureka.org.uk (Children's colour mazes.)
The Forbidden Corner, Leyburn. Telephone: 01969 640638. (Numbers are limited to 120 people an hour; advance booking is required. Tickets can be booked by telephone or at Leyburn Tourist Information Centre on the day of your visit.)
King Edward Street, Hull. (Brick pavement maze.)
The Maize Maze at Cawthorne, near Barnsley. Telephone: 01226 791855. Website: www.maizemaze.co.uk (Seasonal maize maze.)
Poplars Adventure Mega Maze, near Knaresborough. Telephone: 01423 340218. Website: www.maizemaze.com
Temple Newsam House, Leeds LS15 0AD. Telephone: 0113 264 7321. Website: www.leeds.gov.uk (Pavement maze.)

NORTHERN IRELAND
Carnfunnock Country Park, Coast Road, Ballygally, Larne, County Antrim BT40 2QG. Telephone: 028 2827 0541. Website: www.larne.gov.uk/carnfunnock.html
Castlewellan Peace Maze, County Down. (Hedge maze.)

REPUBLIC OF IRELAND
St Regnus Church, Burt, County Donegal.
Dingle Corn Maze, Dingle, County Kerry. Telephone: 0876 109563. Website: www.maizemaze.com
Dunbrody Abbey, County Wexford. (Hedge maze.)
Rathmore Maze, Rathmore Church, Rathmore, County Meath.
Russborough House, Blessington, County Wicklow. Telephone: +353 4586 5239. (Hedge maze.)

The foaming fountain gates in the Darwin Maze at Edinburgh Zoo give the maze puzzle an additional dimension – that of time!

SCOTLAND
Ayrshire Beach Park, Irvine, North Ayrshire. (Concrete path-in-grass maze.)
Blervie House, Nairn, Highland. (Ziggurat hedge maze, private.)
Cairnie Mega Maze, Cupar, Fife. Telephone: 01334 655610. Website: www.cairniefruitfarm.co.uk (Seasonal maize maze.)
Edinburgh Zoo, Edinburgh EH12 6TS. Telephone: 0131 334 9171. Website: www.edinburghzoo.org.uk (The Darwin Maze, consisting of a hedge maze with a pavement maze at the centre.)
Finlaystone House and Gardens, Langbank, Renfrewshire PA14 6TJ. Telephone: 01475 540505. Website: www.finlaystone.co.uk (Granite path-in-grass maze.)
Fishwick Mains Maize Maze, near Berwick-upon-Tweed. Telephone: 01289 386317. Website: www.fishwickmaze.com (Seasonal maize maze.)
Hazlehead Park, Aberdeen. Telephone: 01224 647647. Website: www.aberdeencity.gov.uk (Hedge maze.)
Landmark Centre, Carrbridge, Inverness-shire, Highland PH23 3AJ. Telephone: 01479 841613. Website: www.landmark-centre.co.uk (Raised wooden paths in woodland.)
Murray Maze, Scone Palace, Perth, Perth & Kinross PH2 6BD. Telephone: 01738 552300. Website: www.scone-palace.co.uk (Hedge maze.)
New Town Centre, Irvine, North Ayrshire. (Stained-glass window maze.)
Touchstone Maze, Strathpeffer, near Dingwall, Ross and Cromarty, Highland.
Traquair House, Innerleithen, Peeblesshire, Scottish Borders EH44 6PW. Telephone: 01896 830323. Website: www.traquair.co.uk (Hedge maze.)

WALES
Cim Maze, Abersoch, Gwynedd. Telephone: 07967 050170. Website: www.maizemaze.com
Environmental Maze, Centre for Alternative Technology, Machynlleth, Powys SY20 9AZ. Telephone: 01654 705950. Website: www.cat.org.uk (Hedge maze.)
Heatherton Country Sports Park, near Tenby, Pembrokeshire. Telephone: 01646 651025. Website: www.heatherton.co.uk (Seasonal maize maze.)
Llangoed Hall, Llyswen, Brecon LD3 0YP. Telephone: 01874 754525. Website: www.llangoedhall.com (Hedge maze.)
Roman Legionary Museum, High Street, Caerleon, Newport NP6 1AE. Telephone: 01633 423134. Website: www.nmgw.ac.uk (Roman mosaic labyrinth.)
Rose Hill Quarry Labyrinth, Rose Hill Quarry, near Swansea. NGR: SS 644935. (Gravel path-in-grass maze.)
Techniquest Science Centre, Cardiff. Telephone: 029 2047 5475. Website: www.techniquest.org (Mirror maze.)
Three Cliffs Bay, Pennard, Gower. NGR: SS 539882. (Stone labyrinth.)

The distinctive brick path maze at Chester lies in the gardens beside the medieval Water Tower, which guarded the river approaches, and is overlooked by the Roman city walls. The paths contain three puzzles in contrasting coloured paving; each network has a different layout of junctions.

Index